Battles of the Civil War: Antietam

by Daniel Rosen

Table of Contents

Introduction 2

Chapter 1
Background to Battle 6

Chapter 2
The Bloodiest Day in American History 14

Chapter 3
A Different World 24

Conclusion 29

Solve This Answers 30

Glossary 31

Index 32

Introduction

One issue decided the election for president of the United States in 1860. The issue was slavery. Slavery was legal in the South. It was not legal in the North. The South was afraid the government would pass laws ending slavery.

Four men ran for president that year. Abraham Lincoln won. Lincoln said he would not make laws ending slavery in the South. But he said he did not want slavery to spread to the **territories**. These were newly settled areas that were not yet states.

The South did not believe Lincoln. Southern leaders said if Lincoln won the election, they would **secede** (sih-SEED). Their states would leave the United States. South Carolina did that on December 20, 1860. Other Southern states soon followed.

They united to form a new country. It was called the Confederate States of America, or the **Confederacy** (kuhn-FEH-duhr-uh-see).

The Confederacy created a great **crisis**. A crisis is a dangerous situation. Lincoln said he would keep the **Union** (the whole country) together.

Confederate guns opened fire on Fort Sumter on April 14, 1861. The Civil War had started. The fort surrendered after more than a day of battle.

▲ Abraham Lincoln

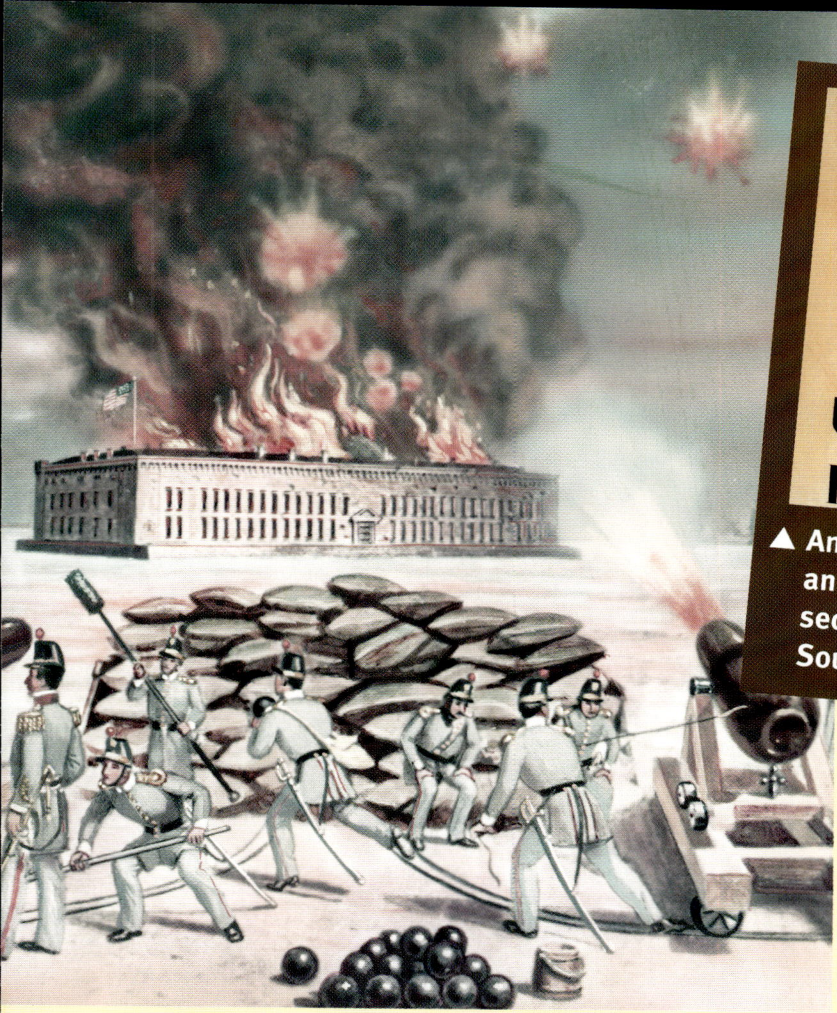

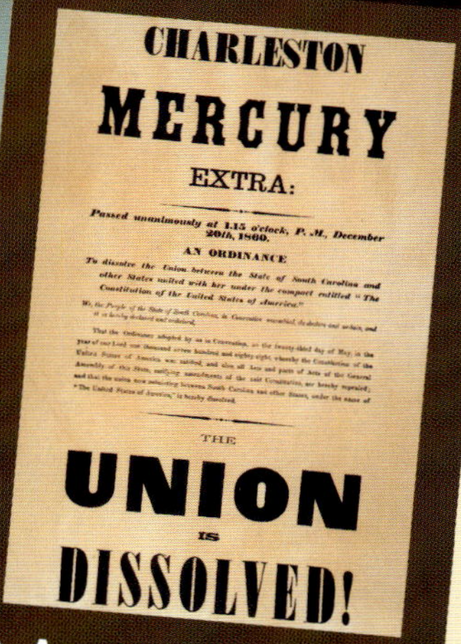
CHARLESTON
MERCURY
EXTRA:

Passed unanimously at 1.15 o'clock, P. M., December 20th, 1860.

AN ORDINANCE

To dissolve the Union between the State of South Carolina and other States united with her under the compact entitled "The Constitution of the United States of America."

THE
UNION
IS
DISSOLVED!

▲ An 1860 newspaper announced the secession of South Carolina.

▲ Soldiers used cannons to destroy Fort Sumter.

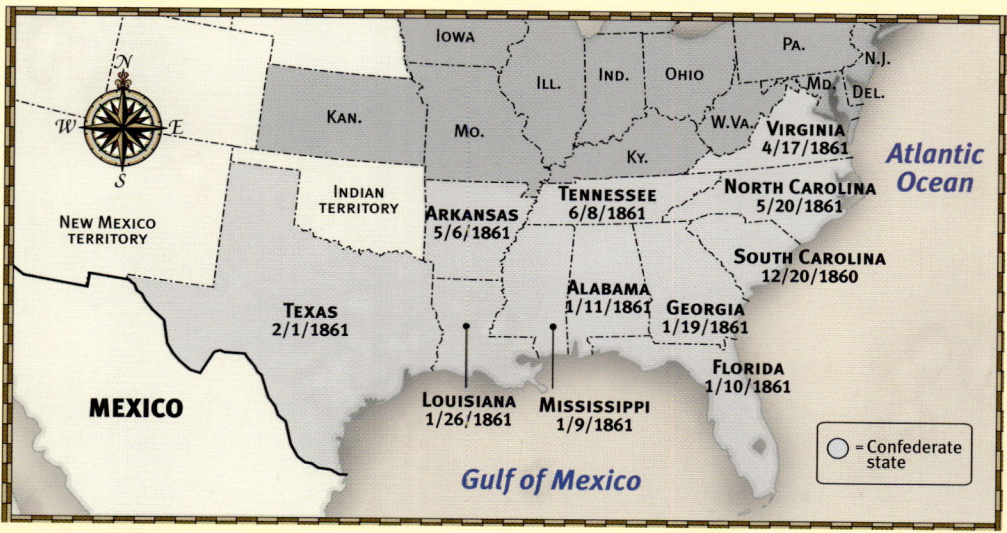

▲ Dates indicate when each state seceded.

INTRODUCTION

Strengths and Weaknesses

In the Civil War, each side had strengths and weaknesses. The North had many more people than the South. It had more men who could become soldiers. It also had more factories, farms, and natural resources. This meant it could make more weapons, uniforms, and other things needed for war. It could grow more food to feed its armies. The North had more railroads, too. That meant it could ship soldiers and supplies more easily.

▲ a Confederate soldier

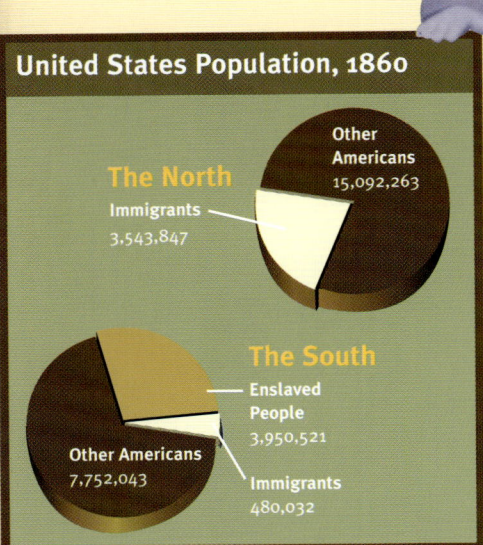

United States Population, 1860

The North
- Immigrants 3,543,847
- Other Americans 15,092,263

The South
- Enslaved People 3,950,521
- Other Americans 7,752,043
- Immigrants 480,032

◀ a Union soldier

But the South had strengths, too. It had much better generals. This fact was not clear at the beginning of the war. But as the war went on, the South's generals were much more successful.

Southern soldiers also were highly **motivated** (MOH-tuh-vay-tehd). They had a very strong reason for fighting the war. Slavery was an important part of the way of life in the South. Southern soldiers were fighting for their way of life.

The South also was defending its own land. Southern soldiers were fighting on land they knew well. Northern armies had to invade the South. They had to fight on land they didn't know. They had to bring supplies from far away.

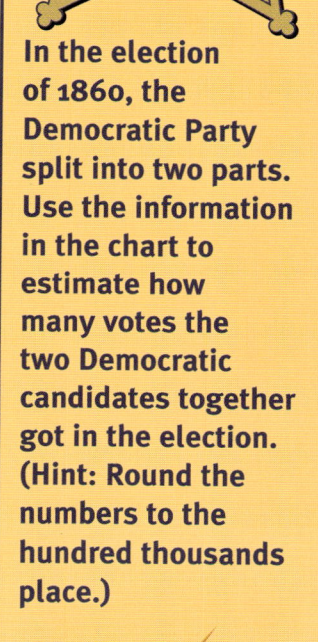

1. SOLVE THIS

In the election of 1860, the Democratic Party split into two parts. Use the information in the chart to estimate how many votes the two Democratic candidates together got in the election. (Hint: Round the numbers to the hundred thousands place.)

MATH POINT

What steps did you follow to get your answers?

Presidential Election, 1860		
Candidate	Political Party	Popular Vote
Abraham Lincoln	Republican	1,865,908
Stephen A. Douglas	Northern Democrat	1,380,202
John Breckenridge	Southern Democrat	848,019
John Bell	Constitutional Union	590,901

CHAPTER 1

Background to Battle

▲ Picnickers in Washington, D.C. rode out to watch the battle. They had to flee when the Union army arrived.

The Union army and the Confederate army had their first battle in July 1861. It took place near Washington, D.C., at a creek called Bull Run. Hundreds of people rode out with the Union army to watch. Many brought picnics along. They were going to watch the battle. Instead they found themselves running for their lives along with the Union soldiers. The Battle of Bull Run showed that the Union army was not ready for war.

Primary Source

On April 9, 1862, President Lincoln sent the following message to General McClellan:

My dear Sir;
Your [message complaining that you do not have enough soldiers and supplies] . . . pain[s] me very much . . . I think it is the [right] time for you to strike a blow. By delay the enemy will . . . gain upon you. . . . And once more let me tell you, it is [important] that you strike a blow . . .
Yours very truly,
Lincoln

After Bull Run, Lincoln wanted a strong leader. He appointed General George McClellan to command the Union army.

At first, McClellan seemed to be an excellent choice to lead the Union army. He inspired his soldiers. He was also good at training and supplying the army. But Lincoln soon noticed something else about McClellan that was not good. McClellan was a very cautious general. He did not attack until he was absolutely sure of success. He did not take risks. Lincoln wanted action. McClellan said that the army was not ready.

▼ General George McClellan

▼ the Battle of Bull Run

CHAPTER 1

Robert E. Lee

General Robert E. Lee led the Confederate armies. He was a very different kind of leader than McClellan.

Robert E. Lee grew up in a military family in Virginia. His father, General "Light Horse" Harry Lee, had been a hero of the American Revolution. Robert E. Lee served in the United States Army most of his career. In 1861, President Lincoln asked Lee to become commander of the Union army. Lee was faced with a hard choice. He was opposed to slavery and secession, but he refused the offer. Lee told the president that his first loyalty was to Virginia. When Virginia left the Union, Lee resigned from the Union army.

Primary Source

There are few, I believe, in this . . . age, who will not agree that slavery . . . is a moral and political evil.
—Robert E. Lee

▲ Robert E. Lee

BACKGROUND TO BATTLE

Lee joined the Confederate army. In 1862, Confederate President Jefferson Davis appointed Lee to command the Army of Northern Virginia. Lee was also made commander of all the armies of the Confederacy.

Like McClellan, Lee inspired great loyalty in his men. But the way that they fought was very different. Lee took risks. He was daring. He often fought battles in which his soldiers were outnumbered. He used surprise and speed in battle to make up for having fewer soldiers.

▲ Jefferson Davis

It's a FACT

Arlington National Cemetery is located in Arlington, Virginia. It is where American war heroes, servicemen, and servicewomen are buried. The grounds of the cemetery were the home of Robert E. Lee. During the Civil War, the Union army took away Lee's land and house.

▲ Arlington National Cemetery

9

CHAPTER 1

Rising and Falling Fortunes

Both sides thought the war would end quickly. Both sides expected to win. There were few major battles in 1861. Neither army was ready to fight battle after battle. In the spring of 1862, the Union army won some important battles. General Ulysses S. Grant won important victories in Kentucky and Tennessee. He captured two Confederate forts. Then, in April 1862, Grant won the Battle of Shiloh (SHY-loh) in Tennessee.

▼ General Ulysses S. Grant

▼ the Battle of Shiloh

BACKGROUND TO BATTLE

▲ Battle of Shiloh

It's a FACT

Shiloh is a Hebrew word that means "place of peace." The Battle of Shiloh was one of the bloodiest battles of the Civil War. More than 20,000 soldiers on both sides were killed or wounded.

The Battle of Shiloh shocked both sides. No battle in American history had ever cost so many lives. Thousands of soldiers died. Thousands more were wounded. The fighting lasted just two days, but they were long and bloody days.

Grant's win in Tennessee cheered people in the North. But people in the South were badly frightened. They worried that the Union army would soon beat them and win the war.

11

Robert E. Lee Strikes Back

In the summer of 1862, Robert E. Lee had the Army of Northern Virginia ready for battle. He quickly moved against the slow-moving McClellan. General Thomas "Stonewall" Jackson helped Lee. Jackson had already won several battles against McClellan. The two armies fought a weeklong battle in Virginia. It was called the Seven Days' Battle. Lee beat McClellan badly. McClellan thought that Lee had more men, so he was slow to attack. But this was not true. McClellan had more than twice the number of soldiers that Lee did. Lee's fast moves were successful. The Confederate army was now able to move close to Washington, D.C. This put the Union capital in danger. Lincoln was angry with McClellan. He thought McClellan should have moved faster and attacked.

▼ Great Britain needed Southern cotton for its textile industry.

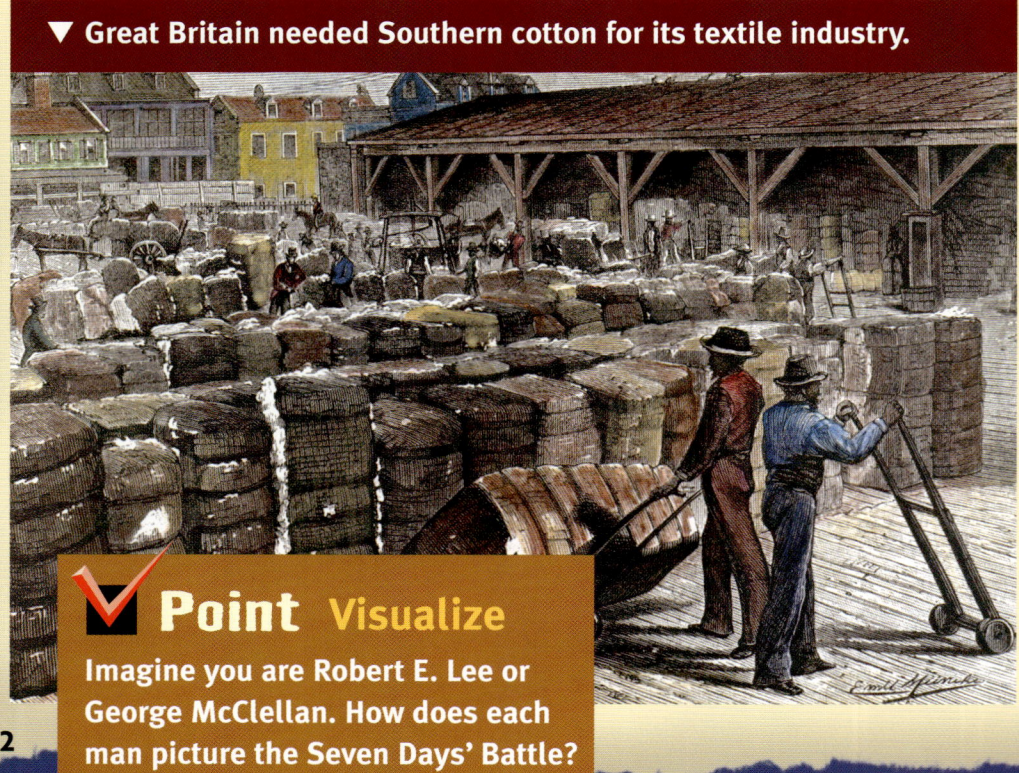

✓ Point Visualize

Imagine you are Robert E. Lee or George McClellan. How does each man picture the Seven Days' Battle?

BACKGROUND TO BATTLE

Diplomacy

The Civil War was more than a military war. It was also a diplomatic war. **Diplomacy** (dih-PLOH-muh-see) is the way countries get along with each other. The Confederacy hoped to get help from Great Britain and France. These two countries needed the cotton grown in the South. They used it for their **textile**, or clothing, industry. Both countries wanted to help the Confederacy. But first they needed to be sure the South had a good chance of beating the North.

It's a FACT

General Thomas "Stonewall" Jackson got his nickname at the Battle of Bull Run in July 1861. Jackson's men were under attack by a strong force of Union soldiers. A Confederate officer could see the attack from nearby. He said that Jackson and his men stood and resisted the attack like a stone wall.

Thomas "Stonewall" ▶ Jackson

13

CHAPTER 2

The Bloodiest Day in American History

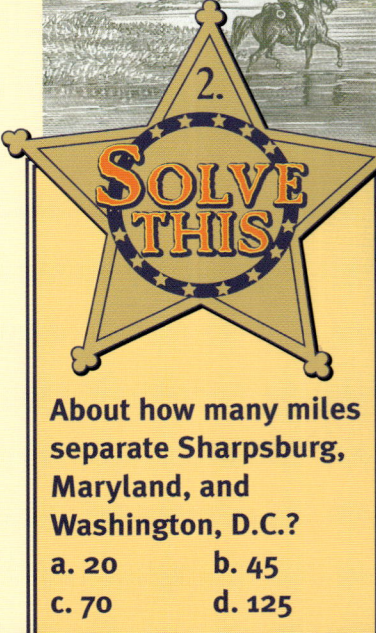

In September 1862, Lee decided to invade the North. He had several reasons for his decision. Lee had fought McClellan's army all summer. He thought he knew how to defeat McClellan. He saw that Confederate victories were causing the Northerners to lose hope. Lee hoped for a big victory in the North. The Northerners might then urge Lincoln to make peace.

Most of the fighting had taken place in Virginia. This was hard on Virginia farmers.

2. SOLVE THIS

About how many miles separate Sharpsburg, Maryland, and Washington, D.C.?
a. 20   b. 45
c. 70   d. 125

MATH POINT

What steps did you follow to get your answer?

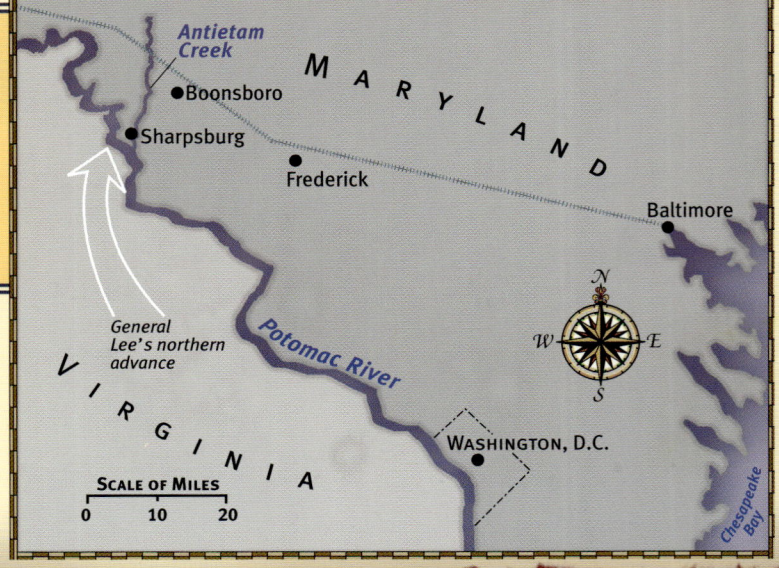

14

▲ **Confederate cavalry crossing the Potomac River on June 11, 1863**

Their farm fields had been turned into battlefields. September was harvest time. Taking the war to the North would protect Southern farms. Also, Lee's army was poorly fed and clothed. But Lee thought the soldiers could **plunder**, or steal, food from Northern farms.

Lee's army crossed the Potomac River. They invaded Maryland. People in Maryland were shocked at how Lee's army looked. Many soldiers were barefoot. Their uniforms were little more than rags. They were hungry and dirty.

The Army of Northern Virginia did not look like much, but its soldiers could fight. And they had a great leader in Robert E. Lee.

Eyewitness Account

A person living in Maryland told a reporter from a Baltimore newspaper that he smelled Lee's army long before he saw them: *"I have never seen a mess of such filthy strong-smelling men . . . They were the roughest set of [men] I ever saw, their . . . hair and clothing matted with dirt and filth."*

CHAPTER 2

▲ Lee's lost order probably looked like this.

The Lost Orders

Battles are sometimes won or lost by a chance happening. On September 9, 1862, Lee gave orders to his commanders. Lee knew that he was badly outnumbered by McClellan. But he also knew how cautious McClellan was. Lee was daring. He split his army in two. He would attack McClellan from two different directions. The danger was that each part of the army would be even more heavily outnumbered. Lee counted on McClellan to move cautiously despite the split forces.

Nine out of ten Confederate soldiers had never owned a slave.

16

THE BLOODIEST DAY IN AMERICAN HISTORY

On September 12, the two armies were moving toward each other. Corporal Barton Mitchell of the Union army was tired. When the army stopped to rest, Corporal Mitchell threw himself under a tree. Much to his surprise, he saw a paper wrapped around three cigars. When he looked more closely, Corporal Mitchell could not believe his eyes. The paper was Lee's orders to his generals. Mitchell brought the orders to headquarters. McClellan and his generals thought they had found the key to victory. Chance had worked in their favor.

THEY MADE A DIFFERENCE

Oliver Wendell Holmes, Jr. was an officer in the Union army. He was badly wounded three times. The last time was at Antietam where no one thought he would survive. He survived and lived to be 94. At the age of 61, Holmes was appointed to the U.S. Supreme Court. He was one of the most important justices ever to serve on the Court.

▲ Oliver Wendell Holmes, Jr.

CHAPTER 2

The Battle of Antietam

On September 17, 1862, the battle took place at last. The two armies met at Antietam Creek. It was near the town of Sharpsburg, Maryland. Different units of each army fought each other across a wide area. They fought a series of skirmishes. One of the most famous of these took place in a 30-acre (12-hectare) cornfield. The field was full of Confederate troops. Union forces attacked. The Confederates returned fire. The battle went on for an hour.

▲ Rufus Dawes

Rufus Dawes was a Union soldier in the battle. He wrote that before the battle, the corn stood taller than the soldiers. "The men were loading and firing with . . . fury," Dawes recalled.

THEY MADE A DIFFERENCE

There were no army nurses in the Civil War. Both armies used volunteers. Many of the volunteers were women. Clara Barton was with McClellan's army at the Battle of Antietam. She worked on the battlefield as the fighting raged. Barton later wrote about what happened as she was giving a wounded soldier a drink:

I bent down to give him a drink. I raised him with my right arm. Then I felt something shake the loose sleeve of my dress. At the same time, the poor fellow sprang from my arms and died. I realized a bullet had passed through my sleeve and hit him. There was no more to be done for him and I left him to rest.

THE BLOODIEST DAY IN AMERICAN HISTORY

"Men . . . were knocked out of the ranks by dozens. But we jumped over the fence, and pushed on, loading, firing, and shouting as we advanced. There was . . . great . . . excitement, eagerness to go forward, and a reckless disregard of life, of everything but victory."

At the end of the battle, the corn had been cut clean to the ground. There was not a stalk left. It was a bare field. This battle became known as "The Cornfield."

It's a FACT

The Battle of Antietam is also known as the Battle of Sharpsburg. Why does the battle have two names? The Union army named battles after nearby waterways. So they called the battle "Antietam" after Antietam Creek, which runs through the battlefield. The Confederacy named battles after nearby towns. The nearest town to the battle was Sharpsburg.

▼ Fierce fighting took place around the Roulette Farm during the Battle of Antietam.

CHAPTER 2

Bloody Lane and Burnside's Bridge

Another part of the battle took place along a half-mile (.8-km) long farm road. Wagon ruts in the ground were several feet (about one meter) deep. The ruts made a good place for Confederate soldiers to stop and fight. Wave after wave of Union troops attacked the Southerners along the road. The outnumbered Southern soldiers kept firing. After four hours, the Union troops were able to drive the Southerners off the road. But hundreds of Union and Confederate troops lay dead. The soldiers named the road "Bloody Lane."

▲ Burnside's Bridge as it looked during the Civil War and as it is today.

▲ The soldiers called this road "Bloody Lane."

THE BLOODIEST DAY IN AMERICAN HISTORY

At the same time, a battle was taking place at a small bridge across Antietam Creek. A group of about 600 Confederate soldiers held off a much larger force commanded by General Ambrose Burnside. Antietam Creek was only about 30 yards (about 27 meters) wide and not too deep. Union soldiers could have easily crossed at other places, but Burnside wanted to claim that bridge. He wanted to drive the Confederates off the bridge. The brave Confederates held out for almost four hours.

The Union won the fight at Burnside's Bridge. But the delay allowed Lee to attack Burnside with soldiers pulled from a different part of the battle. Burnside was trying to take control of the only road out of Sharpsburg. Because of the delay at what became known as Burnside's Bridge, Lee was able to keep control of the road. A day later, control of the road saved his army.

It's a FACT

The Battle of Antietam has not been forgotten. Every year a ceremony is held to remember the day. A candle is lit for each of the more than 23,000 people killed or wounded on both sides.

3. SOLVE THIS

Volunteers make the candles used in the ceremony. Each volunteer can work for 30 hours. If each volunteer can make four candles in an hour, how many volunteers are needed?

MATH ✓ POINT

What steps did you follow to get your answer?

CHAPTER 2

The Killing Fields

The Battle of Antietam ended at nightfall. Only then could both sides begin to count their losses. The final count took several days. Both McClellan and Lee realized that something terrible had taken place along the banks of Antietam Creek. There were more than 23,000 **casualties** at the Battle of Antietam. A casualty is a dead or wounded soldier. The chart shows the losses for each side.

On the morning of September 18, McClellan received **reinforcements** (ree-ihn-FORS-mehnts), or new troops. The Union army now far outnumbered the soldiers that Lee could put in the field. But McClellan was still too cautious. He knew that Lee had split his army. Yet McClellan still believed that the Southerners had more soldiers than he did. So he did not attack. Lee made use of McClellan's caution. He moved his army back across the Potomac River.

4. How many more soldiers did the Union army have than the Confederate army? How many soldiers were killed altogether at the Battle of Antietam?

MATH ✔ POINT

What steps did you follow to get your answer?

Battle of Antietam Casualties

Army	Number of Soldiers in Battle	Killed	Wounded
Union	87,000	2,108	9,549
Confederate	45,000	1,546	9,024

THE BLOODIEST DAY IN AMERICAN HISTORY

Who won the Battle of Antietam? In military terms the battle was a **draw**, or a tie. Both sides lost about the same number of soldiers. But it was easier for the Union army to replace the lost soldiers. With Lee's **retreat**, McClellan proclaimed a great victory. Newspapers in the North celebrated the victory. Only President Lincoln was not happy with the outcome.

▼ The Union and Confederate armies lost thousands of men at the Battle of Antietam.

23

CHAPTER 3

A Different World

President Lincoln believed that McClellan could have finished off Lee's army on September 18. That might have ended the war. Instead, McClellan let Lee get away. Lincoln was angry. He wanted the war to stop. Then he had an idea.

▲ President Abraham Lincoln reading the Emancipation Proclamation

24

Lincoln saw an opportunity after the Battle of Antietam. The press was calling it a great Union victory. Lincoln decided to issue an important document. It was the Emancipation Proclamation. In it, Lincoln freed all the slaves in the Confederacy. This was a powerful law. Finally, slavery had ended.

But few slaves were freed right away. That was because the Union army did not control much of the South. But the Emancipation Proclamation expanded the goals of the Civil War. Now the war was not just being fought to preserve the Union. It was also being fought to end slavery.

Eyewitness Account

Frederick Douglass was the most famous African American in the United States during the Civil War. Douglass had escaped from slavery. He was a leader in the fight against slavery. The Emancipation Proclamation took effect on January 1, 1863. Douglass wrote this about that day:

"The first of January, 1863, was a special day in the progress of American liberty and civilization. It was the turning point in the conflict between freedom and slavery. A death blow has been given to the slaveholding rebellion. We shout for joy that we live [to see this great day]."

✓ Point Reread
Reread pages 24–25. What made Lincoln decide to issue the Emancipation Proclamation?

CHAPTER 3

Effects of the Emancipation Proclamation

The Emancipation Proclamation changed the rules. African Americans had not been allowed to join the Union army. Now they could, and they fought with pride and honor. The Confederacy did not allow slaves to join its army. The North now had more men joining its army and ready to fight.

The Emancipation Proclamation had another effect. It encouraged slaves in the South to run away. The escaping African Americans did not have to reach Northern states. They only had to get as far as Union army lines to find freedom.

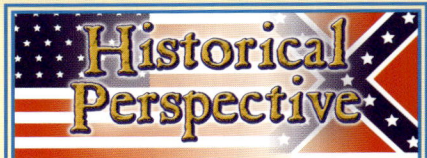

Historical Perspective

The Emancipation Proclamation changed the position of the United States on slavery. At the Constitutional Convention, the Founding Fathers could not agree on slavery and freedom. It took the Civil War to finally solve that conflict. In 1865, President Lincoln urged the Congress to pass the 13th Amendment to the U.S. Constitution. It ended slavery everywhere in the United States.

▲ More than 180,000 African American soldiers served bravely in the war. About 37,000 of them died.

A DIFFERENT WORLD

▲ By the end of the war, nearly one million enslaved African Americans had escaped. That was about one-quarter of all the slaves in the South.

Primary Source

The *New York Tribune* newspaper greeted the news of the Emancipation Proclamation with this editorial written by its editor, Horace Greeley:
GOD BLESS ABRAHAM LINCOLN! . . . *It is the beginning of the end of the rebellion; the beginning of the new life of the nation.*

The Emancipation Proclamation also ended any chance that France and Great Britain would help the Confederacy. Both countries were against slavery. They decided not to help the South.

The Emancipation Proclamation helped Lincoln win more support in the North. Many people wanted Lincoln to take a stronger stand against slavery. The Emancipation Proclamation helped bring the people in the North together. Most Northerners were now committed to winning the war.

The reaction in the South was quite different. People were furious. A Richmond, Virginia, newspaper wrote that the Emancipation Proclamation was "a bid for the slaves to rise in rebellion." To some, it was the end of a way of life.

CHAPTER 3

A Long War

The Civil War raged on for almost three years after the Battle of Antietam. In November 1862, Lincoln, tired of McClellan's excuses, fired the general. His replacements did not do much better. The North had several chances to end the war, but its generals did not act fast enough. The fast-moving and daring Lee could not be stopped. Many people wondered how long the war would last. A war that most people had thought would last no more than a year was still going with no end in sight.

In July 1863, Lee once more invaded the North. Union forces defeated him at the Battle of Gettysburg. But once again, Union forces did not follow up their victory. Lee managed to withdraw to safety. Could anyone ever stop Lee?

In 1864, Lincoln appointed General Ulysses S. Grant commander of the Union army. Grant was not like earlier commanders. He knew that he had to stop Lee. He had to make daring moves. He chased Lee all over Virginia. Lee was skillful enough to make the war last a year longer. But in April 1865, Lee surrendered. The war was finally over.

Paper money first came into use in the United States during the Civil War. The Confederacy was in bad financial condition. It could not get loans to finance the war effort. By 1864, the paper money issued by the Confederacy reached $1 billion. There was so much confederate paper money printed it became almost worthless. There was not enough gold in the treasury to support all the paper currency.

Conclusion

The Battle of Antietam helped decide the outcome of the war. If Lee had won the battle, many things might have changed. It is likely that Great Britain and France would have sided with the Confederacy. Maybe people in the North, tired of the fighting, would have forced Lincoln to make peace. The country would have remained divided. Slavery would have continued, and the history of the United States and the history of the world would have been very different.

Cause	Effect
Lincoln is elected president.	Southern states secede.
The Confederacy attacks Fort Sumter.	The Civil War starts.
McClellan does not attack Lee's army on September 18, 1862.	Lee's army escapes.
Battle of Antietam is seen as a victory for Union forces.	Lincoln issues the Emancipation Proclamation.
Emancipation Proclamation	Ending slavery becomes a goal for the North.
Emancipation Proclamation	African Americans are allowed to join Union army.
Emancipation Proclamation	Great Britain and France are convinced to support the North.

Answers

1. Page 5
The two Democratic candidates together got 2,200,000 votes (rounded).
Stephen A. Douglas (Northern Democrat) = 1,400,000
John Breckenridge (Southern Democrat) = 800,000
 1,400,000 + 800,000 = 2,200,000 total Democratic votes

2. Page 14
c. 70

3. Page 21
Each volunteer can make about 120 candles.
4 candles/hour x 30 hours = 120 candles per volunteer
About 192 volunteers are needed.
23,000 candles needed/120 candles per volunteer = about 192 volunteers

4. Page 22
The Union had 42,000 more soldiers than the Confederacy.
87,000 − 45,000 = 42,000
There were 3,654 soldiers killed at the Battle of Antietam.
2,108 + 1,546 = 3,654

Glossary

casualty (KA-zhul-tee) a dead or wounded soldier (page 22)

Confederacy (kuhn-FEH-duhr-uh-see) the eleven Southern states that declared themselves separate from the United States in 1860 and 1861 (page 2)

crisis (KRY-sihs) a difficult or dangerous situation (page 2)

diplomacy (dih-PLOH-muh-see) the ways countries get along with each other (page 13)

draw (DRAW) a tie (page 23)

motivate (MOH-tuh-vayt) to move someone to action (page 5)

plunder (PLUHN-duhr) to steal (page 15)

reinforcements (ree-ihn-FORS-mehnts) additional soldiers (page 22)

retreat (ree-TREET) to move back (page 23)

secede (sih-SEED) to withdraw from a group or organization (page 2)

territory (TAIR-ih-tor-ee) a settled area belonging to the United States that is not yet a state (page 2)

textile (TEHK-styl) related to the making of cloth (page 13)

Union (YOON-yuhn) the states that stayed loyal to the federal government during the Civil War (page 2)

Index

Army of Northern Virginia, 9, 12, 15
Battle of Antietam, 18, 21–23, 25, 28–29
Battle of Bull Run, 6–7
Battle of Gettysburg, 28
Battle of Shiloh, 10–11
"Bloody Lane," 20
Burnside, General Ambrose, 21
Burnside's Bridge, 21
casualty, 22
Confederacy, 2, 6, 8–10, 12–15, 20, 21, 25–27, 29
crisis, 2
Davis, Jefferson, 9
diplomacy, 13
draw, 23
Emancipation Proclamation, 25–27
Fort Sumter, 2
France, 13, 27, 29
Grant, General Ulysses S., 10–11, 28
Great Britain, 13, 27, 29
Jackson, General Thomas "Stonewall," 12

Lee, General Robert E., 8–9, 12, 14–17, 21–24, 28–29
Lincoln, Abraham, 7, 8, 12, 14, 23–29
Maryland, 15, 18
McClellan, General George, 7–9, 12, 14, 16–18, 22–24, 28
Mitchell, Corporal Barton, 17
motivate, 5
plunder, 15
reinforcements, 22
retreat, 23
secede, 2
Seven Days' Battle, 12
slavery, 2, 5, 8, 25–27, 29
South Carolina, 2
territory, 2
textile, 13
Union, 2, 6–13, 17–23, 25–26, 28
Virginia, 8–9, 12, 14–15, 27–28
Washington, D.C., 6, 12

32